DIAGNOSING AUTISM

A PARENT'S PATHWAY TO ANSWERS

DR. KIMBERLY IDOKO

ALCYONE
BOOKS
Las Vegas, NV

Alcyone Books

This book is for informational and educational purposes only. It is not intended as a substitute for professional legal advice, medical advice, diagnosis, or treatment. Always seek the advice of qualified professionals regarding your specific condition or concern.

Hardcover ISBN: 979-8-335-21039-3

Paperback ISBN: 979-8-335-21039-3

1st Edition, April 2024

CONTENTS

For Lexi

INTRODUCTION

Parenting is a journey full of surprises, each day bringing new discoveries about your child's personality, preferences, and quirks. But what happens when those quirks start to raise questions that no one else seems to have answers for? When my daughter Lexi began to crawl in a way that was unlike any other baby I'd seen, and her words weren't coming as quickly as they had for her older brother, a quiet unease settled in the back of my mind. It was the kind of feeling that's hard to articulate—something just felt 'off.'

Our pediatrician's assurances were meant to soothe my worries. "Lexi's eye contact is perfect," he said, as if that alone could erase the niggling doubts that had taken root. "Children develop at their own pace." It was advice I wanted to believe, yet my instincts whispered a different truth. Deep down, I knew I couldn't ignore what I was seeing. I couldn't shake the feeling that there was more to Lexi's story than what met the eye.

So, I decided to trust my gut. I self-referred Lexi to a developmental pediatrician, where our journey took a pivotal turn. The weeks that followed were a whirlwind of evaluations and tests—parent interviews, surveys, observations, standardized assessments, a brain MRI, genetic testing, and more. Each step brought us closer to the answer we sought, yet each test also added to the weight of uncertainty hanging over us.

Then came the diagnosis: Autism Spectrum Disorder (ASD). Lexi was just two years old. In that moment, I felt the world shift beneath my feet. The word 'autism' came with a wave of emotions—relief at having an answer, fear of the unknown, and a fierce determination to understand what this meant for Lexi's future. It marked the beginning of a journey that would challenge us in ways I hadn't anticipated, but also one that would lead to profound discoveries and a deeper understanding of what it means to be a parent.

The road we've traveled since then has been

anything but straightforward. It's been filled with moments of doubt, times when I questioned my ability to navigate the complexities of Lexi's needs. But it's also been a journey of empowerment, one where I learned to become not just a mother, but an advocate, a teacher, and a tireless researcher in the quest to give Lexi the best possible start.

This book is the culmination of that journey—a guide designed to arm you with the knowledge, tools, and resources necessary to support your child from the earliest signs of autism through to a formal diagnosis and beyond. Autism Spectrum Disorder is complex and multifaceted, and no two children with ASD are exactly alike. Each presents a unique blend of strengths and challenges, making early detection and intervention critical to shaping the best outcomes.

However, the path to diagnosis is often overwhelming, filled with uncertainty and a myriad of emotions that can leave even the most resilient parent feeling lost. That's why I've written *Diagnosing Autism: A Parent's Pathway to Answers*—to provide you with a structured, step-by-step approach to navigate this journey with confidence. Whether you're just beginning to notice developmental differences in your child or are already immersed in the diagnostic process, this book is here to guide you.

In the pages that follow, you'll find detailed information on recognizing early signs and symptoms, understanding the significance of early intervention, and knowing what to expect at each stage of the diagnostic process. This journey may not be one you ever expected to take, but with the right knowledge and support, it's one you can travel with assurance and hope. My hope is that this book will serve as both a roadmap and a companion, helping you to unlock the potential within your child and embrace the path ahead with strength and clarity.

CHAPTER 1

INITIAL CONCERNS & OBSERVATIONS

As a parent, you are often the first to notice when something seems different in your child's development. These initial observations are invaluable in guiding the diagnostic process for autism. Recognizing early signs and behaviors can lead to earlier intervention and better outcomes for your child. Pay close attention to any developmental delays or unusual behaviors your child may exhibit, such as:

COMMUNICATION DIFFICULTIES

Communication challenges are often among the first signs that prompt concern. These difficulties can manifest in various ways:

Delayed Speech Development: Your child may start speaking later than their peers or may have a significantly reduced vocabulary for their age. This could include limited use of words, phrases, or complete sentences.

Lack of Babbling or Pre-Speech Sounds: By the age of one, if your child is not babbling, cooing, or making other vocal sounds, this might be a cause for concern. Babbling is an important milestone that lays the foundation for later speech development.

Difficulty in Maintaining Conversations: Older children with autism might struggle to engage in a two-way conversation. They may talk at others rather than with them, have difficulty staying on topic, or fail to respond to questions appropriately.

Echolalia: Repeating words or phrases that they hear, often out of context or without understanding the meaning. This behavior is common and can sometimes be mistaken for understanding language when it's actually a sign of communication difficulties.

Non-Verbal Communication Issues: Your child may have trouble using or interpreting gestures, facial expressions, or body language. For example, they might not point to objects to show interest or may have a flat or inappropriate facial expression during interactions.

Regression in Language Skills: Some children may develop language skills but then lose them. This regression is a significant red flag and should prompt immediate evaluation by a professional.

SOCIAL INTERACTION ISSUES

Social challenges are another core area of concern in autism. These might be evident through:

Limited Eye Contact: Your child may avoid making eye contact or may not look at people directly, even when being spoken to. Eye contact is a key component of social communication and its absence can be an early sign of autism.

Preference for Solitary Play: Notice if your child prefers to play alone rather than engaging with peers. They may show little interest in playing inter-active games or sharing toys.

Difficulty Understanding Social Cues: Your child may not understand or respond to the social cues of others, such as facial expressions, tone of voice, or body language. This can lead to challenges in forming relationships and engaging in appropriate social behaviors.

Challenges in Forming Friendships: Even with exposure to social situations, your child may struggle to make or maintain friendships. They might show a lack of interest in playing with other children, or they might not understand the concept of give-and-take in relationships.

Unusual Social Responses: Your child may react to social situations in ways that seem odd or inappropriate. This might include not responding to their name, not seeking comfort when distressed, or not showing typical interest in others.

REPETITIVE BEHAVIORS

Repetitive and restricted behaviors are hallmark features of autism. These can include:

Stereotyped Movements: Your child might engage in repetitive movements such as hand-flapping, rocking, spinning, or toe-walking. These behaviors are often performed in a self-stimulatory way and can increase when your child is excited, anxious, or overwhelmed.

Intense Focus on Specific Interests: Your child may develop a deep and narrow interest in certain topics, objects, or activities. This can include a strong attachment to unusual items or an intense focus on a particular subject, like trains or numbers, which might dominate their attention and conversations.

Rigid Routines and Rituals: Your child may insist on specific routines or rituals, such as always eating the same foods, following a strict daily schedule, or becoming extremely distressed when routines are disrupted.

Fixation on Parts of Objects: Instead of playing with toys in the way they are intended, your child may fixate on specific parts of objects, such as spinning the wheels of a toy car rather than driving it.

SENSORY SENSITIVITIES

Children with autism often have unique sensory processing patterns, either being hypersensitive or hyposensitive to sensory input:

Hyperreactivity to Sensory Input: Your child might overreact to certain sensory stimuli, such as covering their ears to block out loud noises, being extremely bothered by certain textures of clothing, or avoiding certain foods due to their texture or taste.

Hyporeactivity to Sensory Input: On the other hand, your child may underreact to sensory experiences. For example, they may not notice when they are injured or may seek out intense sensory input, such as wanting to spin or jump repeatedly.

Unusual Responses to Sensory Experiences: Your child may have unexpected reactions to sensory stimuli, such as being fascinated by light reflections, staring at fans or moving objects, or being unusually interested in certain smells or textures.

Food Sensitivities: Your child may be a very picky eater, rejecting foods based on texture, smell, or even appearance. This can sometimes lead to nutritional concerns if their diet becomes overly restricted.

Temperature Sensitivity: Your child may either overreact or underreact to temperatures. For example, they may not seem to feel cold in chilly weather or may be overly sensitive to warm environments.

OTHER CONSIDERATIONS

While the above categories cover many common signs of autism, it's important to remember that autism is a spectrum, and each child is unique. Additional behaviors that might raise concerns include:

Motor Skill Delays: Delays in gross motor skills (such as walking) or fine motor skills (such as grasping objects) can sometimes accompany autism.

These might include clumsiness or difficulty with coordination.

Emotional Regulation Difficulties: Your child may have frequent meltdowns, intense tantrums, or difficulty transitioning between activities. This can sometimes be mistaken for behavioral issues but may be related to sensory sensitivities or difficulty communicating needs.

Unusual Play Patterns: Your child may play with toys in unconventional ways, such as lining up objects instead of engaging in imaginative play, or repeatedly organizing toys in a specific order.

Inconsistent Responses: Your child may have inconsistent reactions to situations, sometimes appearing to respond typically and other times not. This can be confusing for parents and may make it difficult to pinpoint concerns.

NEXT STEPS FOR PARENTS

If you notice any of these behaviors or developmental delays in your child, it's essential to seek further evaluation:

Document Your Observations: Keep a detailed record of your child's behaviors, including when they started, how often they occur, and any specific triggers or contexts. This information will be invaluable when discussing concerns with healthcare providers.

Consult with a Pediatrician: Share your observations with your child's pediatrician. A thorough discussion can help determine if your child needs further evaluation by a specialist, such as a developmental pediatrician, psychologist, or neurologist.

Early Intervention Services: If your child is under three years old, contact your local early intervention program. Early intervention can provide essential support and therapies that can significantly impact your child's development.

Seek Support: Connect with other parents and support groups. Sharing experiences and resources with others who understand your journey can provide emotional support and practical advice.

Stay Informed: Continue educating yourself about autism and developmental milestones. Knowledge empowers you to make informed decisions and advocate effectively for your child's needs.

By staying vigilant and proactive, you play a crucial role in recognizing early signs of autism and ensuring your child receives the support they need. Your observations are the first step in a journey that can lead to early intervention, better understanding, and improved outcomes for your child.

CHAPTER 2
DOCUMENT SYMPTOMS

Keeping a detailed record of your child's behaviors, communication skills, social interactions, and other concerns is crucial in helping healthcare professionals understand your child's developmental patterns. This documentation can provide invaluable insights during the diagnostic process and guide subsequent interventions.

Documenting your child's symptoms serves several important purposes:

Accuracy in Diagnosis: Detailed records help healthcare professionals get a clearer picture of your child's development over time, leading to a more accurate diagnosis.

Tracking Progress: By keeping detailed notes, you can track your child's progress and identify any patterns or triggers for certain behaviors.

Communication with Professionals: Written documentation provides a clear, organized way to share your concerns and observations with doctors, therapists, and educators.

Empowerment & Advocacy: Having a thorough record allows you to be an informed advocate for your child, ensuring they receive the appropriate support and services.

When documenting symptoms, it's important to be as detailed and specific as possible. Here's a breakdown of what to include:

BEHAVIORS

Observing and recording your child's behaviors can provide important clues about their development. Consider noting the following:

Repetitive Actions: Document any repetitive behaviors such as hand-flapping, rocking, spinning, or other stereotypical movements. Note the frequency, duration, and any potential triggers (e.g., stress, excitement).

Unusual Habits: Record any habits that seem out of the ordinary, such as lining up toys instead of playing with them, repeating specific phrases, or unusual rituals.

Changes Over Time: Keep track of how these behaviors change or evolve over time. Do they become more frequent, less frequent, or remain the same?

Context and Triggers: Note when and where these behaviors occur, and if there are any specific triggers (e.g., certain environments, changes in routine, interactions with others).

COMMUNICATION SKILLS

Communication is a key area to observe, especially in early development. Record details such as:

Speech Development: Track when your child starts speaking, their vocabulary size, and any issues with pronunciation or clarity. Note any regression in language skills.

Response to Gestures: Observe and document how your child responds to non-verbal communication, such as pointing, waving, or nodding.

Use of Language: Pay attention to how your child uses language. Do they ask questions, initiate conversations, or use language mainly to express needs? Note any unusual language patterns, such as echolalia (repeating words or phrases).

Non-Verbal Communication: Note whether your child uses gestures, facial expressions, or body language to communicate. Record instances where they might struggle with understanding or using non-verbal cues.

Conversation Skills: Document how your child engages in back-and-forth conversations, including their ability to stay on topic, respond to questions, and understand the flow of dialogue.

SOCIAL INTERACTIONS

Social development is a significant area of focus in diagnosing autism. Make sure to document:

Interactions with Peers: Observe how your child interacts with other children. Do they play alongside others, engage in cooperative play, or prefer solitary play? Note their ability to share, take turns, and engage in group activities.

Interactions with Adults: Record how your child interacts with adults, including family members, teachers, and strangers. Do they make eye contact, respond to greetings, or initiate conversations?

Understanding of Social Cues: Document instances where your child may struggle to interpret or respond to social cues, such as facial expressions, tone of voice, or body language.

Emotional Responses: Note how your child reacts emotionally to social situations. Do they seem overly shy, anxious, or indifferent? Record any instances of difficulty in managing emotions or understanding the emotions of others.

Play Patterns: Observe and document how your child engages in play. Do they exhibit imaginative play, role-playing, or symbolic play? Note any repetitive play behaviors or unusual interests in specific toys or activities.

OTHER CONCERNS

In addition to the key areas mentioned above, it's important to document any other observations or concerns that might not fit neatly into a specific category:

Sensory Sensitivities: Record any unusual reactions to sensory stimuli, such as light, sound, textures, or tastes. Note if your child seeks out or avoids certain sensory experiences.

Motor Skills: Track any delays or difficulties in fine and gross motor skills, such as difficulty with coordination, walking, or using hands to manipulate objects.

Sleep Patterns: Document your child's sleep habits, including difficulties falling asleep, frequent waking, or unusual sleep behaviors.

Feeding and Eating Habits: Note any picky eating behaviors, food aversions, or preferences for specific textures or flavors.

Behavioral Changes: Keep track of any significant changes in behavior, mood swings, or signs of anxiety or frustration. Include observations of any aggressive behaviors, self-injurious actions, or meltdowns.

Health Concerns: Document any physical health issues, such as gastrointestinal problems, frequent infections, or other medical concerns that may be relevant.

Regression: Note any instances where your child loses previously acquired skills or experiences a regression in development. This could include language, social interaction, or motor skills.

HOW TO DOCUMENT

The method you use to document your child's symptoms should be one that is convenient and easy for you to maintain. Here are some tips:

Journaling: Use a physical journal or notebook to write daily or weekly entries about your child's behavior and development. Include dates, times, and specific details.

Digital Notes: Utilize a notes app on your smartphone or tablet to quickly jot down observations as they happen. Many apps allow you to categorize entries and set reminders.

Behavior Tracking Apps: Consider using specialized apps designed for tracking behaviors, which can help organize data and identify patterns over time.

Photos and Videos: Where appropriate, capture photos or videos of certain behaviors or interactions. This can provide visual documentation that can be helpful for professionals during assessments.

Structured Templates: Create or download structured templates or checklists that prompt you to record specific types of observations regularly.

When meeting with healthcare providers or educators, bring your documentation to provide a comprehensive overview of your child's development:

Summarize Key Points: Before appointments, summarize the most critical observations and concerns to discuss. Highlight any patterns or changes you've noticed over time.

Be Prepared to Provide Examples: Use your documentation to provide specific examples of behaviors or concerns. This helps professionals understand the context and frequency of the behaviors.

Ask Questions: Use your documentation as a basis to ask informed questions about your child's development and potential next steps in the diagnostic process.

Consistent and detailed documentation is a powerful tool in advocating for your child's needs. It helps you stay informed, provides valuable insights to professionals, and ensures that your child receives the appropriate interventions and support. By keeping thorough records, you are taking an active role in your child's developmental journey, ensuring they have the best possible outcomes.

CHAPTER 3
GENERAL PEDIATRICIAN VISIT

When you have compiled your observations, it is crucial to schedule an appointment with your child's primary care physician. This initial consultation is an important step in the diagnostic process, providing a foundation for further evaluation and intervention.

Here's how to make the most of this appointment:

BE THOROUGH AND SPECIFIC
Prepare Your Notes: Bring a detailed record of your observations, including specific examples of behaviors, communication patterns, and social inter-actions. Highlight any concerns that have prompted you to seek medical advice.

Organize Information: Ensure your notes are organized and easy to reference. This could include timelines, frequency of behaviors, and any notable changes over time.

Discuss Observations

Share Detailed Notes: Present your detailed notes to the pediatrician, providing a clear and comprehensive picture of your child's behaviors and developmental progress.

Provide Specific Examples: Use specific examples to illustrate your concerns. For instance, mention if your child avoids eye contact during interactions or if they exhibit repetitive behaviors such as hand-flapping.

Express Concerns

Communicate Significance: Articulate your concerns about your child's development and why you believe further evaluation is necessary.

Ask Questions: Don't hesitate to ask questions about your child's development and what steps can be taken next. This is your opportunity to gain clarity and direction.

DEVELOPMENTAL SCREENING

During the appointment, your pediatrician may conduct a preliminary screening to assess your child's development. This screening typically involves two main components:

MEDICAL HISTORY
Review Medical and Family History: The pediatrician will review your child's medical history, including any past illnesses, developmental milestones, and family history of developmental or neurological conditions.

Discuss Prenatal and Birth History: Information about your child's prenatal development, birth process, and early infancy can provide valuable context for understanding their development.

DEVELOPMENTAL CHECK
Basic Assessment: The pediatrician may perform a basic developmental assessment, which may include observing your child's behavior, communication, and social interactions. They might use standardized screening tools designed to identify developmental delays.

Milestone Evaluation: The assessment will compare your child's development to typical milestones for their age group. This helps to identify any areas where your child may be experiencing delays or challenges.

NEXT STEPS AFTER PEDIATRICIAN VISIT

Follow-Up: Based on the screening results, the pediatrician may recommend follow-up appointments with themselves for further monitoring or refer you to specialists for a more comprehensive evaluation.

The general pediatrician evaluation is a critical step in understanding your child's needs and ensuring they receive the appropriate specialist evaluations and support. By being prepared and proactive, you can help your child access the resources and interventions they need to thrive.

CHAPTER 4
REFERRAL TO SPECIALISTS

If your pediatrician identifies concerns during the initial consultation or developmental screening, they will refer you to specialists who can conduct more comprehensive evaluations.

Specialist evaluations are more specialized than those of a general pediatrician and can help pinpoint specific areas of need and appropriate interventions.

SPECIALIST EVALUATIONS

In-Depth Assessments: Specialists will conduct thorough evaluations using standardized diagnostic tools and techniques to assess your child's development, behavior, and mental health.

Multidisciplinary Approach: Often, a multidisciplinary team will be involved, including developmental pediatricians, psychologists, speech-language pathologists, and occupational therapists, to provide a holistic view of your child's needs.

Intervention Plans: Based on their findings, specialists will recommend specific interventions, therapies, and support services tailored to your child's unique needs.

Ongoing Monitoring: Specialists will also provide guidance on ongoing monitoring and follow-up appointments to track your child's progress and adjust the treatment plan as needed.

Resource Provision: Specialists can connect you with resources, support groups, and educational materials to help you better understand and support your child.

Training: They may offer or recommend training programs for parents to learn effective strategies for managing behaviors and supporting development at home.

By following through with these specialist referrals and gathering thorough documentation, you can ensure that your child receives the most accurate diagnosis and effective interventions possible. This proactive approach is key to supporting your child's development and helping them thrive.

PREPARING FOR SPECIALIST VISITS

Preparing for appointments with specialists involves gathering comprehensive documentation that provides a complete picture of your child's development and behavior. This information is critical for an accurate and thorough assessment.

Here's what you should collect:

Previous Reports: Collect all previous medical reports, including those from your child's primary care physician, any specialists they have seen, and any hospital visits.

Health Records: Include immunization records, growth charts, and any records of illnesses or medical conditions your child has had.

Observations from Teachers: Obtain reports from your child's teachers or caregivers. These reports should include observations of your child's behavior, social interactions, and academic performance in school or daycare settings.

Classroom Behavior: Teachers can provide valuable insights into how your child interacts with peers, follows instructions, and participates in group activities.

Detailed Observations: Bring your own detailed notes about your child's behavior, communication skills, and social interactions. Highlight specific examples and any patterns you have noticed over time.

Journals or Logs: If you have kept a journal or log of your child's behaviors and development, bring these records. They can provide a detailed timeline of your child's progress and any concerns that have arisen.

ADDITIONAL TIPS FOR PREPARING DOCUMENTATION

Organize Chronologically: Arrange documents in chronological order to provide a clear timeline of your child's development and medical history.

Highlight Key Information: Use highlights or notes to draw attention to key observations and concerns that you want the specialist to focus on.

Bring Copies: Make copies of all documents to leave with the specialists. This ensures they have all the necessary information for their evaluations.

If concerns arise during a pediatric visit or developmental screening, specialist referrals allow for a deeper and more precise evaluation of your child's development. These assessments often involve a multidisciplinary team that uses standardized tools to identify strengths, challenges, and support needs, leading to tailored intervention recommendations and ongoing follow-up.

Preparing for these visits is an important step, and includes gathering medical records, prior reports, teacher observations, and your own detailed notes to provide a clear timeline of development. With thorough documentation and specialist input, families can move forward with greater clarity, stronger support plans, and access to the right resources.

CHAPTER 5
MULTIDISCIPLINARY EVALUATION

A multidisciplinary evaluation is a critical step in the diagnostic process for autism. It involves a detailed assessment by a team of professionals who work together to provide a thorough understanding of your child's development, behavior, and needs.

This collaborative approach ensures that all aspects of your child's development are considered, leading to a more accurate diagnosis and effective intervention plan.

A multidisciplinary evaluation typically involves a team of specialists who bring different areas of expertise to the assessment process.

The team may include:

DEVELOPMENTAL PEDIATRICIANS

Role: Developmental pediatricians specialize in the overall development of children. They assess developmental delays, behavioral issues, and other related conditions.

Responsibilities: They conduct physical exams, review medical histories, and evaluate developmental milestones to identify any delays or atypical patterns.

PSYCHOLOGISTS

Role: Psychologists specialize in assessing cognitive, emotional, and behavioral functioning.

Responsibilities: They use various psychological tests and observational techniques to evaluate cognitive abilities, emotional regulation, social skills, and behavior patterns. They may also diagnose co-occurring conditions such as anxiety or ADHD.

SPEECH-LANGUAGE PATHOLOGISTS

Role: Speech-language pathologists (SLPs) focus on communication skills, both verbal and nonverbal.

Responsibilities: They assess language development, speech clarity, understanding and use of language, and social communication skills. They also identify issues such as echolalia, atypical speech patterns, and challenges with pragmatic language.

OCCUPATIONAL THERAPISTS

Role: Occupational therapists (OTs) address fine motor skills, sensory processing, and daily living skills.

Responsibilities: They evaluate motor coordination, sensory sensitivities, and the ability to perform daily activities such as dressing, eating, and playing. They help identify sensory processing issues that may affect behavior and learning.

A multidisciplinary evaluation brings together multiple specialists to build a complete picture of your child's development and support needs. Instead of focusing on a single area, this approach assesses medical history, developmental milestones, cognition, communication, sensory processing, and daily functioning through coordinated input from developmental pediatricians, psychologists, speech-language pathologists, and occupational therapists.

By combining these perspectives, the evaluation

process becomes more thorough, improves diagnostic accuracy, and helps create an intervention plan that reflects your child's full profile rather than isolated symptoms.

CHAPTER 6
PHYSICAL EXAMINATION

Physical examination, which consists of a general and a neurologic examination, is an essential part of the comprehensive evaluation for autism. This examination helps to identify or rule out other medical or neurological conditions that could be contributing to or mimicking autism-like symptoms.

By ensuring a thorough assessment, healthcare providers can more accurately diagnose and address your child's needs.

General Examination

A general examination conducted by a healthcare provider, typically a developmental pediatrician or a general pediatrician, is a first step in the evaluation of autism.

The general exam aims to:

Identify Physical Health Issues: The doctor will check for any physical health problems that could explain or contribute to the symptoms observed. This includes checking for hearing and vision problems, which can sometimes affect communication and social interaction.

Monitor Growth and Development: The doctor will measure your child's height, weight, and head circumference to ensure they are growing and developing appropriately for their age.

Past Medical Issues: The doctor will review your child's medical history, including past illnesses, surgeries, and hospitalizations, to identify any factors that could be affecting their development.

Family Medical History: A review of family medical history can also provide insights into genetic or hereditary conditions that might be relevant.

Vital Signs: The doctor will check vital signs such as heart rate, blood pressure, and temperature.

Basic Examination: This includes examining the skin, eyes, ears, throat, and abdomen to detect any abnormalities or health concerns.

Neurologic Examination

A neurological examination focuses on evaluating the nervous system to ensure there are no underlying neurological issues contributing to the observed symptoms. This examination is critical for understanding your child's motor skills, coordination, and sensory responses.

Motor Skills Evaluation

Gross Motor Skills: The doctor will evaluate your child's ability to perform large movements such as walking and jumping. This helps to identify difficulties with strength or coordination.

Fine Motor Skills: The doctor will assess smaller movements such as picking up objects or buttoning clothes. Fine motor difficulties can affect daily living activities and academic performance.

Coordination Tests: The doctor will observe how well your child can coordinate movements. Tests might include tasks such as touching their nose with their finger, walking heel-to-toe, or catching a ball.

Reflex Testing: The doctor will test the knee-jerk reaction and other involuntary responses to evaluate the brain's functioning.

Sensory Processing: The doctor will evaluate how your child responds to various sensory inputs, such as touch, sound, and light. This helps to identify any sensory processing issues.

Sensory Sensitivities: The doctor will look for signs of hypersensitivity (overreacting to sensory stimuli) or hyposensitivity (underreacting to sensory stimuli). For example, your child may be overly sensitive to loud noises or appear indifferent to pain.

Brain and Nervous System Health: The assessment may include tests to evaluate the overall health of the brain and nervous system. This might involve neuroimaging techniques like MRI or CT scans if there are concerns about structural abnor-malities.

Developmental Reflexes: The doctor will assess primitive reflexes, which are automatic movements that develop during infancy. Persistent primitive reflexes beyond the expected age can indicate neuro-logical issues.

Based on the findings of the physical examination, the healthcare provider may recommend further testing or referrals to other specialists.

These follow-up actions might include:

ADDITIONAL TESTING

Blood Tests: To check for metabolic or genetic disorders that could be contributing to the symptoms.

Hearing and Vision Tests: To rule out sensory impairments that might be affecting communication and behavior.

SPECIALIST REFERRALS

Neurologist: If there are concerns about neurolog-ical conditions, a referral to a pediatric neurologist may be necessary for further evaluation and management.

Geneticist: If there are indications of genetic conditions, a referral to a geneticist for genetic testing and counseling may be recommended.

DEVELOPMENT OF A TREATMENT PLAN

Intervention Strategies: Based on the results of the physical and neurological assessments, the healthcare provider will work with you to develop a comprehensive treatment plan. This plan may include therapies, interventions, and support services tailored to your child's specific needs.

By conducting a thorough physical examination, healthcare providers can ensure that all potential underlying conditions are identified and addressed, leading to a more accurate diagnosis and effective intervention for your child.

This comprehensive approach helps to create a solid foundation for supporting your child's development and well-being.

CHAPTER 7

PARENT INTERVIEWS, QUESTIONNAIRES, & SURVEYS

INTERVIEWS

Parent and caregiver interviews help to create a complete picture of the child's unique profile. Parent interviews cover several areas, including:

CHILD'S DEVELOPMENT

Milestones and Progress: Parents are asked about the child's developmental milestones, such as when they started to crawl, walk, and speak. Specialists look for patterns or delays.

Early Development: Questions may cover prenatal and birth history, and any early signs of developmental differences.

Developmental Changes: Parents provide insights into how the child's skills and abilities have changed or progressed over time.

Behaviors

Specific Habits: Parents are asked to describe specific behaviors observed in the child, such as repetitive actions, unusual habits, or unique interests. This includes details about the frequency, intensity, and context of these behaviors.

Behavioral Changes: Specialists inquire about any significant changes in behavior, such as the onset of new behaviors or the cessation of previous ones.

Social Interactions: Information about how the child interacts with family members, peers, and strangers, including any difficulties in forming or maintaining relationships.

Family History

Genetic History: Questions about the family's medical history, including any genetic disorders, developmental conditions, or mental health issues that may be relevant.

Medical History: Detailed accounts of the child's medical history, including past illnesses, hospitalizations, surgeries, and any chronic health conditions.

Environmental Factors: Information about the child's home environment, parenting styles, and any significant life events that could impact their development.

QUESTIONNAIRES AND SURVEYS

In addition to interviews, parents and caregivers are often asked to complete detailed questionnaires and surveys. These tools are designed to systematically gather information about the child's behavior and development.

BEHAVIORAL QUESTIONNAIRES

Standardized Tools: Commonly used standardized questionnaires, such as the Child Behavior Checklist (CBCL), help quantify aspects of the child's behavior.

Behavioral Patterns: Questions cover a range of behaviors, including social interactions, communication skills, repetitive behaviors, sensory responses, and emotional regulation.

Frequency and Context: Parents indicate how often certain behaviors occur and in what contexts.

DEVELOPMENTAL SURVEYS

Developmental Checklists: These surveys assess various developmental domains, including cognitive, language, motor, and social skills.

Skill Assessment: Parents rate their child's abilities in everyday tasks, such as dressing, feeding, and following instructions.

Comparative Data: The results from these surveys are compared to normative data to identify areas where the child may be lagging behind or excelling.

SOCIAL AND EMOTIONAL ASSESSMENTS

Emotional Well-being: Surveys may include questions about the child's emotional responses, mood stability, and coping mechanisms.

Social Skills: Assessments of social skills and peer

interactions help identify strengths and challenges in building and maintaining relationships.

SENSORY PROCESSING

Sensory Profile: Tools like the Sensory Profile Questionnaire help assess how the child responds to sensory stimuli.

Daily Activities: Questions about how sensory processing affects daily activities, such as eating, dressing, and playing, provide insights into how sensory issues may be addressed in interventions.

Parents and caregivers offer unique perspectives that are essential for a comprehensive evaluation. Their detailed observations and experiences provide context that may not be captured through clinical assessments alone.

This information helps specialists to:

Understand Context: Gain a better understanding of the child's behavior in naturalistic settings and daily routines.

Identify Patterns: Recognize patterns or triggers

that may influence the child's behavior and development.

Develop Personalized Interventions: Create tailored intervention plans that address the specific needs and strengths of the child.

The data collected from interviews and questionnaires is integrated into the overall assessment, contributing to a holistic understanding of the child's developmental profile.

This comprehensive information helps specialists to:

Confirm or Clarify Diagnoses: Use detailed parental insights to confirm or refine diagnostic conclusions based on observed behaviors and standardized test results.

Develop Comprehensive Reports: Compile findings into detailed reports that include parental observations, standardized test results, and professional evaluations.

Inform Treatment Plans: Use the gathered information to develop individualized treatment plans that incorporate family dynamics, environmental factors, and specific developmental needs.

By actively participating in the evaluation process, parents and caregivers play a pivotal role in ensuring that their child receives an accurate diagnosis and appropriate support. Their insights are invaluable in creating a complete picture of the child's unique experiences and needs.

CHAPTER 8
STANDARDIZED TESTING

Standardized testing is a crucial component of the comprehensive evaluation process for autism. These tests provide objective data on your child's development, behavior, and social interactions, helping clinicians to make an accurate diagnosis. The use of standardized diagnostic tools ensures that assessments are consistent, reliable, and grounded in evidence-based practices.

There are two commonly used standardized tests in the autism diagnostic process:

AUTISM DIAGNOSTIC OBSERVATION SCHEDULE (ADOS)

Purpose: The Autism Diagnostic Observation Schedule (ADOS) is a gold-standard, standardized observational assessment used to diagnose autism. It is designed to assess behaviors that are directly related to autism diagnostic criteria, providing valuable insights into your child's social and communicative abilities.

Process: The ADOS involves a series of structured and semi-structured tasks that encourage social interaction, communication, and play. These tasks are carefully designed to elicit behaviors that are indicative of autism. The assessment is tailored to the child's age and language abilities, with different modules used depending on whether the child is nonverbal, minimally verbal, or fluent in speech. During the ADOS, clinicians observe and score specific behaviors, such as eye contact, gestures, verbal and nonverbal communication, imaginative play, and the ability to respond to social prompts. The ADOS is typically conducted in a clinical setting and is designed to be engaging and nonstressful for the child, allowing the clinician to observe natural behaviors.

AUTISM DIAGNOSTIC INTERVIEW-REVISED (ADI-R)

Purpose: The Autism Diagnostic Interview-Revised (ADI-R) is a comprehensive, structured interview conducted with the parents or caregivers of the child. It is designed to gather detailed information about the child's early developmental history and current behavior, providing a deep understanding of the child's developmental trajectory and how it aligns with autism diagnostic criteria.

Process: The ADI-R covers a wide range of topics related to the child's development, including communication skills, social interactions, and repetitive behaviors. The interview is typically lengthy and detailed, often taking several hours to complete. During the ADI-R, the clinician asks parents or caregivers about specific behaviors observed during the child's early years, as well as current behaviors that are characteristic of autism. This includes questions about the child's use of language, ability to engage in social interactions, and presence of repetitive or restrictive behaviors. The information gathered through the ADI-R is used to assess how closely the child's behaviors align with the diagnostic criteria for autism. This tool is particularly valuable in understanding the context and history of the child's development, which may not be fully captured through observation alone.

Standardized tests like the ADOS and ADI-R play a pivotal role in the autism diagnostic process by providing a structured framework for assessing key areas of development and behavior. These tests are used in conjunction with other assessments, such as cognitive and language testing, medical evaluations, and behavioral observations, to create a comprehensive picture of the child's strengths and challenges.

The results of these standardized tests are analyzed in the context of the child's overall developmental profile. Clinicians use the data to identify patterns of behavior that are consistent with ASD and to rule out other developmental or behavioral disorders. The objective nature of standardized testing helps to ensure that the diagnosis is based on consistent criteria and not subjective impressions.

It's important for parents to understand that the

results of standardized tests are one piece of the diagnostic puzzle. While these tests provide critical information, they are part of a broader assessment process that includes clinical judgment, parental input, and other diagnostic tools. The goal is to arrive at a diagnosis that accurately reflects the child's developmental needs and informs the best possible intervention strategies.

CHAPTER 9
BEHAVIORAL OBSERVATIONS

Behavioral observations are a crucial component of the comprehensive evaluation. These observations help specialists understand how your child interacts with their environment and others in various settings.

Key aspects of behavioral observations include:

NATURALISTIC SETTINGS

Observation Locations: Observations may take place in different settings such as the clinic, home, school, or playground.

Purpose: This approach helps capture a range of behaviors and interactions that might not be evident in a single setting.

COMMUNICATION AND SOCIAL INTERACTIONS

Verbal and Nonverbal Communication: Specialists observe how your child communicates, including their use of language, gestures, eye contact, and facial expressions.

Social Engagement: They assess how your child interacts with peers and adults, noting any difficulties in initiating or maintaining social interactions, understanding social cues, and responding to others.

PLAY AND REPETITIVE BEHAVIORS

Play Skills: Observations include how your child plays with toys and engages in imaginative play, as well as their ability to share and take turns.

Repetitive Behaviors: Specialists look for repetitive actions, such as hand-flapping, rocking, or fixations on specific objects or topics, which are common in autism.

SENSORY RESPONSES

Sensory Sensitivities: Observations may include how your child responds to sensory stimuli like lights, sounds, textures, and smells. Specialists look for overreactions or underreactions that may indicate sensory processing issues.

EMOTIONAL REGULATION

Emotional Reactions: Specialists assess your child's ability to regulate emotions, noting any instances of intense emotional reactions, meltdowns, or difficulty coping with changes in routine.

Behavioral observations help specialists see how your child functions in real time across real environments. They reveal patterns in communication, social connection, play, sensory processing, and emotional regulation that may not appear during structured testing. When these observations are gathered across settings like home, school, and clinic, they offer a fuller picture of what your child is navigating day to day. This information helps guide accurate diagnosis and leads to recommendations that fit your child's actual needs.

CHAPTER 10

SPEECH & LANGUAGE ASSESSMENT

Speech and language assessments are integral to diagnosing autism, as communication challenges are a core aspect of the disorder. A speech-language pathologist (SLP) conducts these evaluations to gain a comprehensive understanding of your child's verbal, nonverbal, and social communication skills. This information is essential for developing targeted interventions and support strategies to enhance your child's communicative abilities.

COMMUNICATION SKILLS

The evaluation of communication skills involves a thorough assessment of both verbal and nonverbal communication. The SLP will observe and interact with your child to assess their ability to understand and use language effectively.

VERBAL COMMUNICATION

Use of Words and Sentences: The speech-language pathologist (SLP) will evaluate your child's ability to produce and use words and sentences appropriately for their age. This includes assessing vocabulary and the ability to form coherent sentences.

Expressive Language: Measures how well your child can express their thoughts, needs, and ideas. This includes the use of appropriate grammar, sentence length, and complexity.

Receptive Language: Assesses your child's ability to understand and process spoken language. This includes following directions and under-standing instructions.

Speech Clarity: The SLP will assess how clearly your child can articulate sounds and words. This includes checking for speech sound disorders that can affect intelligibility.

Phonological Awareness: Evaluates your child's awareness of the sound structure of language.

NONVERBAL COMMUNICATION

Gestures: The use of gestures such as pointing or nodding to communicate. The SLP will observe if your child uses gestures appropriately to supplement or replace spoken language.

Facial Expressions: The ability to use facial expressions to convey emotions and reactions. The SLP will evaluate whether your child can appropriately use and interpret facial expressions in different contexts.

Emotional Expression: Observes how well your child expresses emotions like happiness, sadness, or frustration through facial expressions.

Eye Contact: The ability to maintain appropriate eye contact during interactions. The SLP will note whether your child can use eye contact to initiate, maintain, and end conversations.

Joint Attention: Evaluates the ability to share focus on an object or event with another person, which is an important aspect of social communication.

SOCIAL COMMUNICATION

The SLP will assess how your child communicates in various social contexts, including:

INTERACTION WITH PEERS AND ADULTS
Initiating Communication: The ability to start conversations or interactions with peers and adults. This includes initiating greetings, asking questions, and starting play activities.

Maintaining Conversations: The ability to keep a conversation going by taking turns, responding to questions, and staying on topic. The SLP will assess how well your child can maintain back-and-forth exchanges.

Ending Interactions: The ability to appropriately end conversations or interactions. This includes using phrases like "goodbye" or signaling the end of playtime.

UNDERSTANDING AND USING SOCIAL CUES

Interpreting Nonverbal Cues: The ability to understand nonverbal signals from others, such as body language, facial expressions, and tone of voice. The SLP will observe whether your child can accurately interpret these cues in social situations.

Contextual Understanding: Assesses your child's ability to understand and respond to nonverbal cues within different contexts and social settings.

Using Appropriate Social Behaviors: The ability to use socially appropriate behaviors, such as polite greetings, making requests, and showing empathy. The SLP will evaluate whether your child can adjust their behavior based on the social context.

Social Norms and Etiquette: Observes how well your child follows social norms and displays appropriate manners during interactions.

PRAGMATIC LANGUAGE SKILLS

Conversational Skills: The ability to use language effectively in social interactions. This includes knowing how to start, maintain, and end conversations, as well as using language for different purposes (e.g., requesting, informing, commenting).

Perspective-Taking: The ability to understand another person's point of view, feelings, and intentions. The SLP will assess whether your child can consider others' perspectives during interactions.

PLAY AND INTERACTION SKILLS

Imaginative Play: The ability to engage in imaginative or pretend play with peers. The SLP will observe whether your child can create and participate in shared imaginative scenarios.

Cooperative Play: The ability to play cooperatively with others, including sharing, taking turns, and following rules. The SLP will evaluate how well your child can engage in cooperative play activities.

OUTCOME OF THE SPEECH & LANGUAGE ASSESSMENT

Based on the findings of the speech and language assessment, the SLP will provide a detailed report that includes:

Assessment Results: A summary of your child's strengths and challenges in verbal, nonverbal, and social communication.

Diagnostic Information: Information on any identified speech or language disorders, communication delays, or social communication difficulties.

Recommendations: Tailored recommendations for interventions and therapies to address your child's specific communication needs. This may include speech therapy, social skills training, and strategies for improving communication at home and in school.

DEVELOPING A COMMUNICATION PLAN

The information gathered from the speech and language assessment will be used to develop a comprehensive communication plan. This plan will outline specific goals and strategies to help your child improve their communication skills, both verbally and nonverbally.

The plan may include:

Speech Therapy: Regular sessions with a speech-language pathologist to work on articulation, language development, and social communication skills.

Parent Training: Guidance for parents on how to support their child's communication development at home, including tips for encouraging speech, using visual supports, and promoting social interactions.

School-Based Support: Collaboration with educational professionals to implement communication strategies and accommodations in the classroom.

Social Skills Groups: Participation in groups that focus on building social communication skills through structured activities and peer interactions.

By thoroughly evaluating and addressing your child's communication needs, the speech and language assessment plays a vital role in helping your child develop effective communication skills, fostering better social interactions, and enhancing their overall quality of life.

CHAPTER 11
COGNITIVE & DEVELOPMENTAL TESTING

Cognitive and developmental testing is a critical part of the comprehensive evaluation process for autism. These assessments provide detailed insights into your child's intellectual abilities, developmental progress, and adaptive functioning. The results help to identify strengths and areas that may require support, informing the development of tailored intervention plans.

INTELLECTUAL ASSESSMENT

Intellectual assessment, or cognitive testing, aims to evaluate your child's intellectual abilities and identify any developmental delays. This assessment involves a series of standardized tests that measure various aspects of cognitive functioning, including:

GENERAL INTELLIGENCE

IQ Tests: Commonly used intelligence tests, such as the Wechsler Intelligence Scale for Children (WISC) or the Stanford-Binet Intelligence Scales, provide an overall measure of your child's cognitive abilities. These tests assess different domains, including verbal comprehension, perceptual reasoning, working memory, and processing speed.

Verbal Comprehension: Assesses your child's ability to understand and use language.

Perceptual Reasoning: Evaluates problem-solving skills and the ability to understand and interpret visual information.

Working Memory: Measures the capacity to hold and manipulate information in the mind over short periods.

Processing Speed: Assesses the speed and accuracy of cognitive processing.

SPECIFIC COGNITIVE SKILLS

Attention & Concentration: Tests that evaluate your child's ability to focus and maintain attention on tasks.

Sustained Attention: Assesses the ability to maintain focus on a task over an extended period.

Selective Attention: Measures the ability to focus on specific information while ignoring distractions.

Divided Attention: Evaluates the ability to manage multiple tasks simultaneously.

Memory: Assessments that measure both short-term and long-term memory, including the ability to recall information and perform memory tasks.

Short-Term Memory: Evaluates the ability to remember information for a brief period.

Long-Term Memory: Assesses the ability to store and retrieve information over longer periods.

Executive Functioning: Tests that assess higher-order cognitive processes, such as planning, organizing, problem-solving, and decision-making.

Planning & Organization: Evaluates the ability to plan and execute tasks in a structured manner.

Problem-Solving: Measures the ability to identify solutions to complex problems.

Decision-Making: Assesses the ability to make informed choices and judgments.

Academic Skills: Some cognitive assessments include tests of academic skills, such as reading, writing, and mathematics.

Reading Comprehension: Assesses the ability to understand and interpret written text.

Mathematical Reasoning: Measures the ability to solve mathematical problems and understand numerical concepts.

Writing Skills: Evaluates the ability to express ideas in written form.

DEVELOPMENTAL MILESTONES

Developmental Scales: Tools like the Bayley Scales of Infant and Toddler Development or the Mullen Scales of Early Learning assess a range of developmental milestones, including motor skills, language, cognitive abilities, and social-emotional development.

Motor Skills: Evaluates gross and fine motor development.

Language Development: Assesses receptive and expressive language skills.

Cognitive Abilities: Measures problem-solving and cognitive processing.

Social-Emotional Development: Evaluates social interactions and emotional regulation.

ADAPTIVE FUNCTIONING

Adaptive functioning refers to the practical, everyday skills needed to live independently and interact effectively with others. This assessment looks at your child's ability to perform daily living activities and helps to understand their level of independence and self-care skills. Key areas of adaptive functioning include:

Daily Living Skills

Self-Care: Evaluates your child's ability to perform basic self-care tasks, such as dressing, feeding, bathing, and toileting. This includes assessing whether your child can complete these tasks independently or requires assistance.

Dressing: Measures the ability to select and put on clothes appropriately.

Feeding: Assesses the ability to eat independently and use utensils.

Bathing: Evaluates the ability to maintain personal hygiene.

Toileting: Measures the ability to use the bathroom independently.

Household Tasks: Assesses the ability to perform simple household chores, such as cleaning, cooking, and organizing personal belongings.

Cleaning: Evaluates the ability to clean and maintain living spaces.

Cooking: Assesses basic cooking skills and the ability to prepare simple meals.

Organizing: Measures the ability to keep personal belongings organized and tidy.

SOCIAL SKILLS

Interpersonal Skills: Evaluates how your child interacts with others, including peers, family members, and adults. This includes assessing the ability to form and maintain relationships, communicate effectively, and understand social cues.

Forming Relationships: Measures the ability to establish and maintain friendships.

Effective Communication: Assesses verbal and nonverbal communication skills in social interactions.

Understanding Social Cues: Evaluates the ability to interpret and respond appropriately to social signals.

Community Participation: Assesses your child's ability to engage in community activities, such as attending school, participating in recreational activities, and navigating public spaces.

School Participation: Measures the ability to engage in school activities and interact with classmates and teachers.

Recreational Activities: Assesses participation in hobbies, sports, and other leisure activities.

Navigating Public Spaces: Evaluates the ability to travel and function in community settings, such as using public transportation or shopping.

CONCEPTUAL SKILLS

Functional Academics: Evaluates practical academic skills.

Reading Skills: Assesses the ability to read and comprehend functional texts, such as instructions and signs.

Writing Skills: Measures the ability to write for

practical purposes, such as filling out forms or writing notes.

Math Skills: Evaluates the ability to perform basic math tasks, such as counting money and telling time.

Problem-Solving & Decision-Making: Assesses the ability to solve everyday problems and make decisions that impact daily life.

Problem-Solving: Measures the ability to identify problems and develop practical solutions.

Decision-Making: Assesses the ability to make informed choices about personal and daily living activities.

OUTCOME OF COGNITIVE & DEVELOPMENTAL TESTING

The results of cognitive and developmental testing provide a detailed profile of your child's intellectual abilities, developmental progress, and adaptive functioning. This information is used to:

Identify Strengths & Weaknesses: Highlight areas where your child excels and areas that may require additional support or intervention.

Diagnose Developmental Delays: Confirm or rule out developmental delays and other cognitive or learning disabilities.

Inform Educational Planning: Develop individualized education plans (IEPs) and other educational accommodations tailored to your child's unique needs.

Guide Intervention Strategies: Design targeted intervention programs that address specific areas of need, such as cognitive skills, adaptive functioning, and social development.

Monitor Progress: Track your child's development over time to evaluate the effectiveness of interventions and adjust strategies as needed.

By thoroughly assessing both cognitive and adaptive functioning, specialists can provide a comprehensive understanding of your child's developmental profile. This holistic approach ensures that all aspects of your child's growth and development are considered, leading to more effective and personalized support.

After completing the evaluation, the multidisciplinary team will compile their findings into a comprehensive diagnostic report.

This report will include:

Detailed Observations: Summaries of the behavioral observations across different settings.

Test Results: Results from standardized tests and assessments.

Diagnostic Conclusion: A diagnosis based on the collective findings, including any co-occurring conditions.

Recommendations: Tailored recommendations for interventions, therapies, and support services to address your child's specific needs.

The multidisciplinary evaluation is designed to provide a holistic view of your child's development, ensuring that all aspects of their behavior and functioning are considered. This thorough approach leads to a more accurate diagnosis and a personalized plan to support your child's growth and development.

After completing the multidisciplinary evaluation process, the team will provide detailed feedback and a formal diagnosis. This phase is critical for understanding the results of the assessments and developing a plan to support your child's development effectively.

CHAPTER 12
DIAGNOSTIC REPORT

The multidisciplinary team compiles their findings into a comprehensive diagnostic report. This report is a crucial document that provides an in-depth overview of your child's assessment and serves as a foundation for developing a tailored intervention plan.

The diagnostic report typically includes:

Symptoms Observed

Behavioral Symptoms: Detailed descriptions of the behaviors observed during the evaluations, including repetitive behaviors, social interaction difficulties, and communication challenges.

Developmental Symptoms: Information on developmental delays or atypical patterns observed in motor skills, cognitive abilities, and adaptive functioning.

Sensory Symptoms: Observations of sensory processing issues, such as hypersensitivity or hyposensitivity to sensory stimuli.

TEST RESULTS

Standardized Test Scores: Results from cognitive, developmental, and language assessments, including IQ scores, language proficiency, and adaptive functioning levels.

Behavioral Assessments: Scores and interpretations from behavioral questionnaires and observational tools, such as the Autism Diagnostic Observation Schedule (ADOS) and the Autism Diagnostic Interview-Revised (ADI-R).

Medical and Neurological Findings: Results from physical and neurological exams, highlighting any medical conditions or neurological issues identified during the assessment.

OVERALL FINDINGS

Summary of Evaluations: A comprehensive summary that integrates findings from all assessments, providing a holistic view of your child's strengths and challenges.

Diagnostic Criteria: An explanation of how your child's symptoms and test results align with the diagnostic criteria for autism spectrum disorder, based on established guidelines such as the DSM-5 (Diagnostic and Statistical Manual of Mental Disorders).

DIAGNOSIS DISCUSSION

Following the compilation of the diagnostic report, you will have a detailed discussion with the multidisciplinary team. This meeting is an opportunity to review the findings, ask questions, and gain a clear understanding of your child's diagnosis.

Key components of the diagnosis discussion include:

CRITERIA MET

Specific Characteristics & Behaviors: The team will explain the specific characteristics and behaviors that led to the autism diagnosis, such as social communication difficulties, restrictive and repetitive behaviors, and sensory processing issues.

Diagnostic Criteria: An overview of the diagnostic criteria met according to established guidelines, ensuring you understand the basis for the diagnosis.

OBSERVATIONS

Key Findings: The team will highlight key findings from the evaluations and assessments, providing insights into your child's developmental profile.

Strengths & Challenges: A discussion of your child's strengths, such as areas of strong cognitive abilities or social skills, as well as challenges that need to be addressed.

Based on the diagnosis, the multidisciplinary team will provide tailored recommendations designed to support your child's development and well-being.

These recommendations typically include:

INTERVENTIONS

Specific Therapies: Recommendations for specific therapies, such as speech therapy, occupational therapy, applied behavior analysis (ABA), and social skills training, to address identified needs.

Support Services: Information on additional support services, such as counseling, behavioral therapy, and family support programs, to provide comprehensive care for your child.

TREATMENT PLAN

Comprehensive Plan: A detailed treatment plan that outlines short-term and long-term goals for your child's development. This plan will include specific objectives, strategies, and timelines for achieving these goals.

Educational Support: Recommendations for educational support, such as developing an Individualized Education Plan (IEP) or 504 Plan, to ensure your child receives appropriate accommodations and support in the school setting.

Home & Community Strategies: Practical strategies for supporting your child's development at home and in the community, including routines, communication techniques, and sensory accommodations.

Monitoring and Follow-Up: A plan for regular monitoring and follow-up appointments to track your child's progress and make adjustments to the treatment plan as needed.

COLLABORATIVE APPROACH

The feedback and diagnosis phase is a collaborative process between the multidisciplinary team and the family. It is designed to empower you with the knowledge and tools needed to support your child's development effectively.

Here's how the collaborative approach works:

FAMILY INVOLVEMENT

Active Participation: Encourage active participation from parents and caregivers during the discussion, ensuring your insights and concerns are considered in the treatment plan.

Education & Training: Provide education and training for parents to help them understand the diagnosis, the recommended interventions, and how to implement strategies at home.

ONGOING COMMUNICATION

Regular Updates: Maintain open lines of communication with the multidisciplinary team, allowing for regular updates on your child's progress and any necessary adjustments to the treatment plan.

Support Network: Connect with support networks, including local and national autism organizations, support groups, and online communities, to gain additional resources and support.

By the end of the feedback and diagnosis phase, you will have a comprehensive understanding of your child's developmental profile, a clear diagnosis, and a detailed, actionable plan to support their growth and well-being. This collaborative, informed approach ensures that your child receives the best possible care and support tailored to their unique needs.

CHAPTER 13
AFTER DIAGNOSIS

Receiving a diagnosis of autism for your child can be a pivotal moment, providing clarity and direction for addressing their needs. The next steps after the diagnosis involve creating a comprehensive support plan, considering various therapies, and connecting with support resources. These steps are crucial for ensuring your child receives the necessary interventions and support to thrive.

DEVELOP A SUPPORT PLAN

Creating a tailored education and support plan is a critical first step in ensuring your child receives the appropriate interventions, accommodations, and resources needed to thrive. This process involves collaboration with a team of professionals, including educators, therapists, and medical providers who understand your child's unique needs.

A well-developed support plan not only addresses academic and behavioral challenges but also fosters your child's overall development and well-being.

Here's how to approach this essential task:

Individualized Education Plan (IEP)

An Individualized Education Plan (IEP) is a legally binding document that outlines the specific educational services and supports your child will receive in school. It is designed for children who have been formally diagnosed with a disability that impacts their ability to learn in a traditional classroom setting.

Assessment & Goals:

Initial Evaluation: Start by collaborating with educational professionals to conduct a thorough assessment of your child's strengths and challenges. This evaluation may include academic testing, observations, and input from teachers, therapists, and you as the parent.

Goal Setting: Based on the assessment, develop specific, measurable goals that are tailored to your child's unique needs. These goals should be realistic yet challenging, designed to help your child progress academically, socially, and emotionally.

Annual Reviews: IEP goals are reviewed and updated at least once a year, allowing the plan to evolve as your child grows and their needs change.

ACCOMMODATIONS & MODIFICATIONS: Tailored Support: Work with the IEP team to identify accommodations and modifications that will help your child succeed in the classroom. Accommodations might include preferential seating, extended time for tests, or the use of assistive technology such as speech-to-text devices.

Modifications: If necessary, adjust the curriculum to match your child's learning level and pace. This might involve simplifying assignments, using alternative teaching methods, or providing additional instructional support.

Behavioral Supports: Include strategies and interventions to address any behavioral challenges your child may face, ensuring they can participate fully in the classroom environment.

SPECIALIZED INSTRUCTION:

One-on-One Support: Implement specialized instruction methods, such as one-on-one support from a special education teacher or paraprofessional, to address your child's individual learning needs.

Small Group Instruction: Small group settings can provide more focused and personalized teaching, allowing your child to receive the attention and support they need to master key skills.

Curriculum Adjustments: Tailor the curriculum to your child's learning style and abilities, ensuring they can engage with the material in a meaningful way.

HOME SUPPORT STRATEGIES

Supporting your child's development at home is just as important as the support they receive in school. By creating a nurturing and structured home environment, you can reinforce the skills and strategies your child is learning in their educational setting.

ROUTINE & STRUCTURE

Daily Schedule: Establish a consistent daily routine to provide stability and predictability, which can help reduce anxiety and improve your child's ability to manage transitions between activities.

Visual Schedules: Use visual schedules or charts to help your child understand and anticipate daily activities, reducing uncertainty and helping them feel more in control of their environment.

Consistent Expectations: Maintain consistent expectations for behavior and responsibilities at home, helping your child develop a sense of security and routine.

COMMUNICATION TECHNIQUES

Clear Language: Use clear, simple language when communicating with your child, breaking down instructions into manageable steps.

Visual Supports: Enhance communication by using visual supports, such as picture cards, symbols, or written words, to aid in understanding and expression.

Positive Reinforcement: Reinforce positive behaviors and communication efforts with praise, rewards, or other forms of positive reinforcement, encouraging your child to continue developing their skills.

BEHAVIOR MANAGEMENT

Positive Behavior Support: Implement positive behavior support strategies to address challenging behaviors and encourage positive actions. This might include using reward systems, setting clear boundaries, and providing immediate feedback.

Proactive Strategies: Identify potential triggers for challenging behaviors and develop proactive strategies to prevent them, such as creating calming spaces or offering choices to help your child feel more in control.

Collaboration with Professionals: Work with behavioral specialists or therapists to develop individualized behavior plans that can be implemented consistently across home and school settings.

EMOTIONAL SUPPORT

Social-Emotional Learning: Integrate social-emotional learning activities at home, such as role-playing social situations, teaching coping strategies, and encouraging emotional expression.

Building Resilience: Help your child build resilience by teaching problem-solving skills, fostering a growth mindset, and providing opportunities for success and mastery.

Family Involvement: Involve the entire family in supporting your child's development, creating an inclusive and supportive environment that fosters understanding and collaboration.

Developing a comprehensive support plan that addresses your child's unique needs requires careful planning, collaboration, and ongoing adjustment. By working closely with educators, therapists, and other professionals, and by implementing consistent support strategies at home, you can help your child reach their full potential and thrive in all areas of life.

CHAPTER 14
THERAPIES

Various therapies can play a transformative role in your child's development, helping them acquire essential skills, improve their quality of life, and navigate the world with greater ease and confidence. Each therapy is designed to address specific areas of need, tailored to your child's unique challenges and strengths. Here's a closer look at some of the most commonly used and effective therapies for children with autism:

APPLIED BEHAVIOR ANALYSIS (ABA)

Foundational Approach: Applied Behavior

Analysis (ABA) is widely regarded as one of the most effective therapies for children with autism. It is based on the principles of learning theory and focuses on improving specific behaviors, such as social skills, communication, and adaptive behaviors, through positive reinforcement and structured techniques.

Targeted Skill Development: ABA programs break down complex skills into smaller, manageable tasks, which are taught systematically and reinforced with positive rewards. This method helps children learn and retain new skills by providing consistent and immediate feedback.

Behavior Management: ABA also addresses challenging behaviors by identifying the triggers and functions of these behaviors, then developing strategies to replace them with more appropriate alternatives.

Personalized Goals: ABA programs are tailored to your child's individual needs, taking into account their specific challenges, strengths, and interests. The therapy is highly customizable, with specific goals set based on the initial assessment of your child's abilities.

Continuous Assessment: Progress is continuously monitored and assessed, allowing the program to be adjusted as your child achieves milestones or encounters new challenges. This ongoing evaluation ensures that the therapy remains aligned with your child's evolving needs.

Parent Involvement: Parents are often involved in ABA therapy, receiving training to reinforce strategies at home and to help maintain consistency across different environments.

SPEECH THERAPY

Verbal & Nonverbal Communication: Speech therapy is designed to enhance your child's ability to communicate effectively, whether through verbal language or nonverbal means. For children with speech delays or difficulties, this therapy focuses on articulation, vocabulary development, and improving the clarity and coherence of speech.

Social Communication: Beyond just words, speech therapy also addresses pragmatic language skills—how your child uses language in social contexts. This includes understanding and using greetings, making requests, taking turns in conversation, and interpreting nonverbal cues like facial expressions and body language.

Alternative Communication Methods: For children with limited or no verbal speech, Augmentative and Alternative Communication (AAC) methods provide alternative ways to communicate. This can include picture exchange communication systems (PECS), speech-generating devices, or sign language.

Empowering Communication: AAC tools empower children by giving them a means to express their needs, thoughts, and emotions, which can significantly reduce frustration and improve their ability to interact with others. AAC can also be used as a bridge to developing verbal skills, offering a foundation for later speech development.

Customizable Options: Speech therapists work closely with families to select and customize AAC systems that best fit the child's abilities and communication needs, ensuring that the tools are both accessible and effective.

OCCUPATIONAL THERAPY (OT)

Daily Living Skills

Fine Motor Skills: Occupational therapy focuses on enhancing your child's fine motor skills, which are crucial for tasks such as writing, buttoning clothes, and using utensils. Strengthening these skills helps children become more independent in their daily lives.

Functional Independence: OT also addresses practical life skills, such as dressing, feeding, grooming, and other activities of daily living (ADLs). These are skills that children need to perform independently as they grow, and improving them can lead to greater self-reliance and confidence.

Customized Interventions: Therapists tailor interventions to your child's specific needs, incorporating activities that are engaging and directly related to their goals. This might include games that improve hand-eye coordination or exercises that build muscle strength and control.

Sensory Integration Therapy

Understanding Sensory Processing: Many children with autism experience sensory processing issues, where their brain has difficulty responding appropriately to sensory inputs such as sounds, lights, textures, or movement. Sensory Integration Therapy helps children learn to process and respond to sensory stimuli in a more regulated and adaptive manner.

Therapeutic Activities: Through carefully designed activities, children are exposed to different sensory experiences in a controlled environment, allowing them to gradually build tolerance and improve their responses. This might involve using swings, weighted blankets, or textured materials to help the child adjust to sensory inputs.

Improving Focus and Behavior: By addressing sensory challenges, this therapy can help reduce anxiety, improve focus and attention, and decrease behaviors associated with sensory overload, such as meltdowns or avoidance.

SOCIAL SKILLS TRAINING

GROUP SESSIONS

Structured Social Interaction: Social skills training often takes place in group settings, where children have the opportunity to practice interacting with peers in a structured and supportive environment. These sessions are designed to mimic real-life social situations, providing a safe space for children to learn and rehearse appropriate social behaviors.

Peer Interaction: Group sessions encourage children to engage with others, fostering friendships and teaching the importance of cooperation, sharing, and turn-taking. The group dynamic helps children learn from one another and provides opportunities to observe and model positive social interactions.

ROLE-PLAYING & MODELING

Practical Learning: Role-playing exercises allow children to practice specific social scenarios, such as greeting someone new, asking for help, or joining a group activity. These exercises help demystify social rules and provide clear examples of how to behave in various situations.

Behavioral Modeling: Therapists and peers model appropriate social behaviors, demonstrating how to initiate conversations, interpret social cues, and resolve conflicts. Children can then practice these behaviors in a guided setting, receiving feedback and encouragement as they learn.

Building Confidence: Social skills training not only teaches specific skills but also builds confidence in social settings. As children become more comfortable with social interactions, they are more likely to engage positively with peers and adults outside of therapy.

INTEGRATING THERAPIES FOR HOLISTIC DEVELOPMENT

The therapies outlined above are often most effective when integrated into a comprehensive treatment plan that addresses all aspects of your child's development.

Collaborating with a multidisciplinary team of professionals ensures that each therapy complements the others, providing a well-rounded approach to supporting your child's growth.

Parental Involvement

Active Participation: Your involvement in your child's therapy is crucial. By learning the techniques and strategies used in therapy sessions, you can reinforce these skills at home and in everyday situations, creating a consistent and supportive environment for your child.

Home Programs: Many therapists provide home-based programs or exercises that can be done outside of formal therapy sessions, helping to strengthen the gains made during therapy.

Regular Monitoring & Adjustment

Ongoing Evaluation: Regularly monitor your child's progress in each therapy, and be open to adjusting the plan as needed. As your child grows and their needs evolve, the focus of therapy may shift to address new challenges or build on emerging strengths.

Collaborative Efforts: Ensure that all therapists and educators involved in your child's care are communicating and collaborating to provide a cohesive and integrated approach to your child's development.

By engaging in these therapies, you can help your child build essential life skills, enhance their ability to communicate and interact with others, and improve their overall quality of life. With the right support, your child can reach their full potential, navigating the world with greater independence and confidence.

SUPPORT RESOURCES

Connecting with local and national support resources can provide invaluable assistance and a sense of community.

LOCAL & NATIONAL SUPPORT GROUPS
Parent Support Groups: Joining parent support groups allows you to share experiences, gain insights, and receive emotional support.

Online Communities: Online forums and social media groups offer opportunities to connect with a broader community of parents.

ADVOCACY ORGANIZATIONS
Information & Resources: Organizations like Autism Speaks and the Autism Society provide

information on autism, including research updates, educational materials, and resource guides.

Advocacy & Support: These organizations advocate for the rights of individuals with autism and offer support services, such as legal advice and assistance with navigating the education system.

COMMUNITY RESOURCES

Local Programs: Explore local programs and services, such as recreational activities, respite care, and specialized camps, that cater to children with autism.

Healthcare Providers: Connect with healthcare providers who specialize in autism and related conditions.

GOVERNMENT & NON-PROFIT SERVICES

Early Intervention Programs: For younger children under the age of three years old, early intervention programs provide essential services, including therapy and developmental support, to address developmental delays.

Special Education Services: Public schools

offer special education services and resources to support children with autism. Work closely with school administrators and special education teams to access these services.

IMPLEMENTING THE SUPPORT PLAN

Once a support plan is in place, ongoing monitoring and adjustments are essential to ensure it remains effective and responsive to your child's needs.

REGULAR REVIEWS

IEP Meetings: Schedule regular meetings with your child's educational team to review progress, update goals, and make necessary adjustments to the plan.

Therapy Progress Reports: Maintain regular communication with therapists to monitor your child's progress and meet at least every six months to discuss any changes needed in their therapy programs.

ADJUSTMENTS BASED ON PROGRESS

Flexible Goals: Be prepared to adjust goals and

strategies based on your child's progress and changing needs.

Parent & Caregiver Feedback: Provide feedback to the multidisciplinary team on what is working well and what challenges remain, ensuring a collaborative approach to your child's care.

By developing a comprehensive support plan, engaging in various therapies, and connecting with support resources, you can create a nurturing and effective environment for your child's development. These steps will help you navigate the journey after diagnosis, ensuring your child receives the support and interventions they need to thrive.

RESOURCES

Recognizing and addressing autism symptoms early can make a profound difference in your child's development and quality of life. Early intervention is key, and being equipped with the right knowledge and resources will empower you to make informed decisions for your child's well-being. This book is designed to guide you through the complexities of autism, providing you with the tools and confidence needed to navigate this journey.

As you embark on or continue along this path, remember that you are not alone. There are numerous resources, communities, and professionals ready to offer support, advice, and understanding. Building a strong network of support is crucial for both you and your child. The following resources are invaluable starting points, offering a wealth of information, community connections, and access to services tailored for families navigating autism.

WEB RESOURCES

Autism Speaks:

Website: autismspeaks.org

Overview: Autism Speaks is a leading organization dedicated to promoting solutions for individuals with autism and their families through advocacy, support, and research. The website offers extensive resources, including toolkits for different stages of life, information on early signs of autism, and guidance on navigating the diagnosis process. It also provides a searchable directory of services and support networks, as well as opportunities to get involved in advocacy efforts.

The Autism Society:
Website: autism-society.org
Overview: The Autism Society is one of the oldest and most respected grassroots organizations focused on improving the lives of individuals with autism. The website offers educational resources, information on autism across the lifespan, and connections to local affiliates that provide support services. Their National Helpline is also available to offer personalized support and connect you with local resources.

Centers for Disease Control and Prevention (CDC) - Autism Spectrum Disorder (ASD):
Website: cdc.gov/ncbddd/autism
Overview: The CDC provides scientifically based information on Autism Spectrum Disorder, including early signs and symptoms, screening and diagnosis, and the importance of early intervention. The website also offers resources for parents, caregivers, and professionals on managing autism and promoting healthy development. Additionally, the CDC's "Learn the Signs. Act Early." program provides free developmental monitoring tools to help track your child's progress.

Wrightslaw:
Website: wrightslaw.com
Overview: Wrightslaw is an excellent resource for understanding special education law, advocacy, and the rights of children with disabilities. The site offers comprehensive infor-

mation on navigating the educational system, developing Individualized Education Programs (IEPs), and ensuring that your child receives the services they are entitled to under the law. It's a critical tool for parents seeking to advocate for their child's educational needs.

National Institute of Mental Health (NIMH) - Autism Spectrum Disorder:
Website: https://www.nimh.nih.gov/health/topics/autism-spectrum-disorders-asd
Overview: The NIMH offers a wealth of information on Autism Spectrum Disorder, including research findings, treatment options, and ongoing studies. This site is a valuable resource for those interested in the latest scientific developments in autism and mental health.

Autism Navigator:
Website: autismnavigator.com
Overview: Autism Navigator provides a series of web-based courses and tools aimed at helping parents, caregivers, and professionals understand and support children with autism. The platform offers interactive, video-based resources that demonstrate early signs of autism and effective intervention strategies.

SAMPLE SOCIAL STORIES

Social stories are short narratives that describe social situations and outline appropriate responses or behaviors. They are designed to help children with autism understand and navigate social interactions and new experiences. These stories can be customized to fit specific situations that your child might encounter, such as visiting the doctor, starting a new school, or handling a change in routine.

The purpose of these sample social stories is to provide you with examples of how to create personalized stories that guide your child through various social scenarios. By using social stories like these, you can help your child feel more prepared and confident when facing new or challenging situations.

Sample Social Story 1: Going to the Doctor

Title: My Visit to the Doctor

Story:

Tomorrow, I will go to the doctor. The doctor is there to help me stay healthy. When I arrive, I will sit in the waiting room with my mom/dad. There might be other people waiting too. While I wait, I can look at a book or play with a toy.

When it's my turn, the nurse will call my name. I will walk to the exam room with my mom/dad. The nurse might check my weight and height, and that's okay. The doctor will come in next and ask how I am feeling. The doctor might use some tools to look in my ears, eyes, and mouth. These tools help the doctor see how I am doing.

If I feel nervous, it's okay to tell my mom/dad or the doctor. The doctor will listen to me. After the check-up, the doctor might give me a sticker for being brave. Then, I will go home with my mom/dad. Going to the doctor helps me stay healthy!

Sample Social Story 2: Starting a New School

Title: My First Day at a New School

Story:

Next week, I will start at a new school. This is a big change, and it's okay to feel excited and a little nervous. I will meet new teachers and new friends. When I arrive at school, my teacher will show me where to put my backpack. I will sit at a desk just like at my old school.

There will be new classmates to meet. I can smile and say, 'Hi, my name is [Child's Name].' My teacher will tell us what we will do for the day. We might have reading time, math, and play-time. If I have a question, I can raise my hand and ask the teacher.

At lunchtime, I will eat in the cafeteria with other students. I can sit with someone new and ask if I can join them. After lunch, we will go back to class. The school day will end, and I will go home. Each day, I will learn new things and meet more friends. My new school will become a place where I feel comfortable and happy."

SAMPLE SOCIAL STORY 3: HANDLING A CHANGE IN ROUTINE

Title: When Plans Change

Story:

Sometimes, plans can change, and that's okay. Today, I was supposed to go to the park, but it started to rain. Instead of the park, we will stay inside and play a game or watch a movie.

It's okay to feel disappointed when plans change. I can tell mom/dad how I feel. We will think of something fun to do at home. Even though I can't go to the park today, I can still have a good time. Maybe the rain will stop, and we can go another day.

When things don't go as planned, I can try to stay calm and flexible. There are many fun things to do, even when plans change. I can always find something to enjoy!

HOW TO CREATE YOUR OWN SOCIAL STORIES

Step 1: Identify the Situation

Choose a specific social situation or experience that your child needs help understanding or navigating. This could be anything from visiting a new place to learning how to share with others.

Step 2: Break Down the Situation

Divide the situation into simple, manageable steps. Consider the key points your child needs to know and what they might be feeling at each stage.

Step 3: Write the Story

Write a short, clear narrative that explains the situation and the expected behaviors or responses. Use simple language and first-person perspective to make it relatable for your child.

Step 4: Include Visuals (Optional)

Adding pictures or illustrations can help reinforce the story. You can use photos of the actual places or people involved, or simple drawings that represent the scenario.

Step 5: Read and Review

Read the social story with your child multiple times before the event or situation occurs. Encourage them to ask questions and discuss how they feel about the story.

Step 6: Reinforce and Reflect

After the situation occurs, revisit the social story with your child. Reflect on how things went and discuss any differences or similarities to the story.

AFTERWORD

Navigating an autism diagnosis can be filled with uncertainties, but it is also a journey of discovery, resilience, and profound personal growth. With the right resources, supportive networks, and a steadfast belief in your child's potential, this journey can open up new possibilities for understanding, connection, and advocacy.

When I first noticed that Lexi's development was different from other children her age, it was unsettling. The eventual diagnosis of autism brought a mix of relief and challenge—it was the beginning of a path that would test my resilience but also strengthen my resolve to advocate for Lexi's needs. Through this experience, I learned an invaluable lesson: as parents, we are our children's strongest advocates. No one knows your child like you do, and your instincts are powerful tools in navigating this journey.

There will be moments of doubt, frustration, and heartache, but there will also be moments of triumph, understanding, and joy as you witness your child's progress and see them find their unique place in the world. The tools and resources shared in this book are designed to empower you to take charge of your child's journey with confidence and hope. Utilize these tools, connect with communities of support, and never hesitate to ask for help or seek second opinions.

You are not alone on this journey; countless other parents have walked similar paths and are ready to offer support, advice, and understanding. Remember that the journey through an autism diagnosis is not just about overcoming challenges—it's about celebrating the small victories, embracing the unique perspectives your child brings, and discovering new strengths within yourself.

This path may not be the one you originally envisioned, but it is rich with opportunities for connection, learning, and growth. Stay informed, seek out support, and continue to trust your instincts. Your dedication, love, and persistence will guide you and your child through this journey, helping them to thrive and reach their full potential.

Together, you and your child will navigate the complexities of autism, discovering new ways to communicate, connect, and celebrate each step forward. With the right support and determination, you and your child can undoubtedly flourish.

ABOUT THE AUTHOR

Dr. Kimberly Idoko is a Yale-, Penn-, and Stanford-educated neurologist and attorney who works with families navigating neurodevelopmental differences. She brings a rare combination of clinical neuroscience, systems literacy, and lived experience as a mother to the question parents are rarely given time to ask: what is actually happening inside my child's brain?

She is a board-certified physician who cares for thousands of patients each year. She is also the founder of Special Parent Coach, where she helps parents interpret early neurological signs and understand how modern systems shape outcomes.

She lives in Los Angeles with her family.

instagram.com/drkimberlyidoko

tiktok.com/@drkimberlyidoko

drkimberlyidoko.substack.com